JUNIOR GREAT BOOKS

SERIES 3

BOOK ONE

◆ ◆ ◆

The interpretive discussion program that moves

students toward excellence in reading comprehension,

critical thinking, and writing

JUNIOR GREAT BOOKS®

SERIES 3   BOOK ONE

THE GREAT BOOKS FOUNDATION
A nonprofit educational organization

Junior Great Books® is a registered trademark of the Great Books Foundation. Shared Inquiry™ is a trademark of the Great Books Foundation. The contents of this publication include proprietary trademarks and copyrighted materials, and may be used or quoted only with permission and appropriate credit to the Foundation.

Published and distributed by

THE GREAT BOOKS FOUNDATION
A nonprofit educational organization

35 East Wacker Drive, Suite 400

Chicago, IL 60601

CONTENTS

"One day the heart and banza will be one."

THE BANZA

Haitian folktale
as told by Diane Wolkstein

On the island of Haiti, there once lived a
little tiger named Teegra and a little goat named
Cabree. Usually tigers and goats are enemies, but
these two were best friends.

They had met during a thunderstorm when
they had each run into the same cave for shelter.
The storm had lasted all night, and when they
came out in the morning, everything seemed
strange to them, for they had come out of the
cave by a different entrance and were lost.

They were both quite small, lonely, and afraid.
They looked at each other.
Cabree brayed, "Be-be. . . ."

Teegra roared, "Rrr. . . ."

"Do you want to be friends?" Cabree asked.

"Now!" Teegra answered.

So they wandered over the countryside, playing together, sharing whatever food they found, and sleeping close to each other at night for warmth.

Then one morning, they found themselves in front of the cave where they had first met.

"rrRRRRR!"

Cabree turned. But it was not Teegra who had roared.

"RRRRRRrrr-rrRR!"

It was a roar of another tiger.

"Mama! Papa! *Auntie*!" Teegra cried joyfully as three huge tigers bounded out of the bushes.

Cabree ran into the cave without waiting. After a while, Teegra went to find Cabree, but Cabree refused to come out of the cave, so Teegra went home with his family.

The next morning, Teegra went to the cave alone.

"Cabree!" he called. "I brought you a banza."

Cabree poked her head out of the cave.

"A *ban-za*? What's that?"

"A little banjo," Teegra said. "It belonged to my uncle, but I want you to have it—so it will protect you."

"How will the banza protect me?" Cabree asked.

"Auntie says, 'The banza belongs to the heart, and there is no stronger protection than the heart.' When you play the banza, Auntie says to

place it over your heart, and 'one day the heart and banza will be one.' "

"Is that true?"

"Oh, Cabree, I don't really know, but I know I shall not forget you."

Teegra placed the banza around his friend's neck, then he turned to go.

"Where are you going?" Cabree asked.

"Home!" Teegra answered, and the little tiger ran back to his family without stopping.

Cabree stepped out of the cave so she could see the banza more clearly. It was a beautiful

banza, and when the sun shone on it, it gleamed.
Cabree held the banza over her heart. She
stroked it gently. A friendly, happy sound
came out. She stroked it again—and again
—and before she realized it, she was
trotting through the forest, humming
to herself and stopping now and
then to play a tune on the banza.

•••

One afternoon Cabree came to a spring. She wanted to drink, but she was afraid the banza would get wet, so she took it off and carefully laid it down in the bushes. As she drank the cool sweet water, she heard a low growl behind her.

"rrrRRrrr. . . ."

Turning quickly, Cabree saw four large hungry tigers. Cabree wanted to leap across the stream and run away, but the banza was in the bushes behind the tigers. No! She would not leave the banza Teegra had given her.

Slowly and fiercely Cabree walked toward the banza.

Another tiger appeared. Now there were five.

Cabree kept walking.

"Where are you going?" the leader shouted.

Cabree reached the bushes. She picked up the banza and hung it around her neck. Then she turned to the tigers. Five more jumped out of the bushes.

Now there were ten!

"What have you put around your neck?" asked the leader.

And Cabree, trying to quiet her thundering, pounding heart, brought her foreleg to her chest and, by mistake, plucked the banza.

"A musician!" said the chief, laughing. "So you wish to play us a song?"

"No!" said Cabree.

"No?" echoed the leader. And all the tigers took a step closer to Cabree.

Teegra! Cabree wanted to shout. But Teegra was far away, and she was alone, surrounded by the tigers. No, she was not completely alone. She still had the banza Teegra had given her.

Cabree's heart beat very fast, but in time to her heartbeat, she stroked the banza. She opened her mouth, and a song came out. To her own surprise, it was a loud, low, ferocious song:

Ten fat tigers, ten fat tigers,
Cabree eats tigers raw.
Yesterday Cabree ate ten tigers;
Today Cabree eats ten more.

The tigers were astonished.

"Who is Cabree? And where did you learn that song?" demanded the chief.

"I am Cabree." Cabree answered in a new deep voice, and noticing how frightened the tigers looked, she added, "And that is *my* song. I always sing it before dinner."

The tiger chief realized that three of his tigers had suddenly disappeared.

"Madame Cabree," he said, "you play beautifully. Permit me to offer you a drink."

"Very well," said Cabree.

"Bring Madame Cabree a drink!" he ordered
the two tigers closest to him, and as they started
to leave he whispered, "and don't come back."

Five tigers stared at Madame Cabree.

Cabree stared back. Then she stroked her banza
and sang, a little slower, but just as intently:

Five fat tigers, five fat tigers,
Cabree eats tigers raw.
Yesterday Cabree ate ten tigers;
Today Cabree eats five more.

"Oh! Oh-h-h! Something dreadful must have happened to my tigers," said the leader. "You." He motioned to the two tigers nearest him. "Go fetch Madame Cabree a drink." And again he whispered, "And don't come back."

Now only three tigers quaked before Madame Cabree. Cabree sang again:

Three fat tigers, three fat tigers,
Cabree eats tigers raw.
Yesterday Cabree ate ten tigers;
Today Cabree eats three more.

When she finished her song, only the leader remained. Cabree began:

One fat tiger—

"Please," whispered the leader, "please let me go. I promise no tiger will ever bother you again."

Cabree looked at the trembling tiger. All she had done was to play the banza and sing what was in her heart. So Teegra's auntie was right. Her heart had protected her. Her heart and her banza.

"Please!" begged the leader. "I'll do whatever you wish."

"Then go at once to Teegra, the little tiger who lives near the cave. Tell Teegra: 'Today Cabree's heart and the banza are one.'"

"Yes, yes," said the tiger. "Today Cabree's heart and the banza are one." And the tiger chief ran off to find Teegra.

...

With her banza gleaming around her neck,
Cabree went trotting through the forest. But
every now and then, she would stop. She would
stroke her banza and sing, for her heart would
have a new song.

"Is it possible that someone is trickier than I?"

THE MAN WHOSE TRADE WAS TRICKS

Georgian folktale as told by
George and Helen Papashvily

There was, there was, and yet there was
not, there was once a king who, like all kings,
wanted to believe he was the trickiest man
in the whole world.

During the day when his court stood near to
applaud each word he spoke, he felt sure of this.
But at night when sleep was slow he worried.

Is it possible, is it really possible, he would
think to himself, that there might be someone
who is trickier than I?

Finally he could endure it no longer, and he
called his viziers together.

"Go," he commanded them, "and find the trickiest man in my kingdom and bring him here before me. I will match myself against him. If he loses he must be my slave for life."

The viziers set out and in their travels they met many clever men—such clever men, in fact, that they refused to go back and match themselves against the king for no better reward than a promise they might be slaves.

The viziers grew desperate.

At last one night they came through a fertile valley bordered with thick forests into the street of a poor village. Now this village, you should know, was not poor because it was a lazy village or a stupid village. It was poor because the king owned the valley and all the forest beyond. Each year he took such a heavy rent that no matter how hard the villagers worked when harvest time came, nothing was left for them but the middlings of their own wheat and a few crooked tree stumps.

But poor as this village was, they knew how to act like rich men. They called the viziers to the best supper they could cook and afterward, for their entertainment, built a campfire and told stories.

...

As the evening sharpened itself to a point, the viziers noticed that one man, Shahkro, was better than all the rest at guessing riddles and remembering poems and describing his adventures.

"Let us see if he will go with us and match himself against the king," whispered the viziers to each other.

At first when they asked Shahkro he refused, but finally after some persuasion he said, "I will go with you, but I will go just like this. Without my hat and without my *cherkasska*."

And exactly that way they brought him before the king.

"Sit down," the king said. "So you think you are the trickiest man in my kingdom?"

"Tricking is my trade," Shahkro answered.

"Try to trick me then," the king commanded. "But I warn you," he added, "it cannot be done for I am so tricky myself."

"I can see that," Shahkro said. "I wish I had known all this before. I would have come prepared. As it was,

26

I left in such a hurry I didn't stop for my hat or my *cherkasska*, to say nothing of my tools."

"What tools?"

"Why, the tools I use for tricking people."

"Go and get them."

"That's not so easy. Naturally, as I'm sure you know from your own experience, I can't just bundle them together as though they were something ordinary. I need wagons."

"Wagons?" said the king. "How many wagons?"

"About a hundred with a hundred horses to pull them."

"Take them from my stable but come right back."

"Certainly," Shahkro said. "With luck I should have everything loaded in five or six months."

"Five or six months?"

"I'll need to bring *all* my tools if I must trick you."

"Well, come back as soon as you can."

"By the way," Shahkro said when the wagons were brought and he was ready to drive off, "if I can't trick you I know I must be your slave for the rest of my life, but just suppose I win, what then?"

"But you can't win," the king told him.

"I know I can't, but suppose I did."

"Well, what do you want?"

"Something you wouldn't miss if you gave it to me."

"I agree," said the king.

Shahkro went home at a fast trot, called all the villagers together,

gave them each a horse and wagon, and
working side by side they sowed and harvested
a crop large enough to last them for ten years.

"At least we have this much out of it," Shahkro
said, when the last load of grain came creaking
into the barn. "Now bring me all the empty
wineskins you can find."

When these were collected, Shahkro blew
them full of air and piled them on the wagons
and rode back to the palace.

The king was waiting impatiently for him
in the great hall, surrounded by all his nobles
dressed in their richest costumes.

"Let us begin," the king said.

"I must unpack my tools," Shahkro told him.

"I will send servants to do that," the king said.

While they were waiting the king's dog ran
into the room and, noticing a stranger was
there, he came over and sniffed Shahkro's legs
to make his acquaintance.

Shahkro bent his head and blew very lightly in the dog's ear. The dog, of course, in turn licked Shahkro's ear.

"This is awful news!" Shahkro jumped up from his chair. "Awful! Where's my hat? Where's my coat? I beg you loan me the fastest horse in your own stable. My dear wife whom I left well and happy yesterday, is dying."

"How do you know?" cried the king.

"How does he know?" cried the court.

"Your dog, as you saw, whispered it in my ear just now."

Everyone was sorry and the king ordered the best horse in his stable saddled, a full-blooded black Arabian, and Shahkro rode away home.

He stayed there long enough to sell the horse for a good price and buy a black donkey.

Then he put the horse's saddle and bridle on the donkey and went back to town.

···

The king was waiting in the courtyard, and when he saw Shahkro jogging along he cried out, "Where is my horse?"

"Horse?" Shahkro said. "Horse! Oh King, have your joke at my expense. I am only a poor man. But I never thought you would do a thing like this to me. Send me home to my sick wife on a horse that changes himself back and forth to a donkey as it suits his pleasure."

"That's impossible," the king said. "I've had that horse for five years."

"Impossible or not," Shahkro answered, "here I am the same as I started out for home five days ago. Here is the same bridle in my hands. Here is the same black animal under me. And it's a donkey."

The king looked at the saddle and at the bridle. He ran his hand over the donkey's flank. "Well, all I can say in apology is that he never did it while I rode him. But let's forget all that. When are you going to try to trick me?"

"Right now," Shahkro said. "Sit down. Answer me a question. You claimed you were a trickster. Did you ever use any tools?"

"No."

"Then why did you think I would? So there I tricked you once. In all the years you had your dog, did he ever talk to you?"

"No."

"Then why did you think he would talk to me? I tricked you twice. In all the years you had your black horse, did he ever turn into a donkey for you?"

"No."

"Then why should he for me? There I tricked you three times. Now pay me and I will go."

The king saw he had one last chance to redeem his reputation as a trickster so he said, "Remember, for your reward I promised only what I wouldn't miss. You must choose something I never use or otherwise I would miss it. Now what shall it be?"

"Your head," Shahkro answered.

When the king heard this he began to shake and turn so green that Shahkro took pity on him. "Wait," he said, "I will take another reward. Because on second thought you do use your head. It keeps your hat from lying on your shoulders. Give me instead your forest and all the fields around it for my village people to use for their own."

"Certainly," said the king, and he called his viziers and sealed the agreement right there and gave it to Shahkro. "And now I don't want to keep you for I know you are anxious to get home."

Shahkro went back to his village and in honor he lived there all his life.

As for the king, after that he didn't have to worry anymore whether or not he was the trickiest man in the world, so I suppose he slept very well. Or maybe because he was a king he found a new worry to keep him awake.

THE FISHERMAN AND HIS WIFE

Brothers Grimm

There was once a fisherman and his wife who lived together in a hut by the seashore. The fisherman went out every day with his hook and line to catch fish, and he angled and angled.

One day he was sitting with his rod, looking into the clear water, when suddenly down went the line to the bottom of the water. When he drew it up, he found a great fish on the hook.

The fish said to him, "Fisherman, listen to me. Let me go. I am not a real fish but an enchanted prince. What good shall I be to you if you land me?

I shall not taste good. So put me back into the water again and let me swim away."

"Well," said the fisherman, "no need of so many words about the matter. As you can speak, I had much rather let you swim away." So he cast him back into the sea. Then the fisherman went home to his wife in the hut.

"Well, husband," said the wife, "have you caught anything today?"

"No," said the man. "That is, I did catch a huge fish, but as he said he was an enchanted prince, I let him go again."

"Did you not wish for something?" asked his wife.

"No," said the man. "What should I wish for?"

"Oh dear!" said the wife. "It is so dreadful always to live in this hut. You might as well have wished for a little cottage. I daresay he will give it to us. Go and be quick."

When he went back, the sea was green and yellow and not nearly so clear. So he stood and said:

Oh, man of the sea, come listen to me,
For Alice, my wife, the plague of my life,
Has sent me to ask a boon of thee.

Then the fish came swimming up and said, "Now then, what does she want?"

"Oh," said the man, "my wife says that I should have asked you for something when I caught you. She does not want to live any longer in the hut and would rather have a cottage."

"Go home," said the fish. "She has it already."

So the man went home and found, instead of the hut, a little cottage, and his wife was sitting on a bench before the door. She took him by the hand and said to him, "Come in and see if this is not a great deal better." They went in, and there was a little sitting room and a beautiful little bedroom, a kitchen and a larder, with all sorts of

furniture, and iron and brassware of the very best. And at the back was a little yard with chickens and ducks, and a little garden full of green vegetables and fruit.

"Look," said the wife, "is not that nice?"

"Yes," said the man. "If this can only last, we shall be happy the rest of our days."

"We will see about that," said his wife.

All went well for a week or fortnight. Then the wife said, "Look here, husband, the cottage is really too small. I think the fish had better give us a larger house. I should like very much to live in a large stone castle. So go to your fish, and he will send us a castle."

"Oh, my dear wife!" said the man. "The cottage is good enough. What do we want a castle for?"

"Go along," said the wife. "He might just as well give it to us as not. Do as I say."

The man did not want to go, and he said to himself, "It is not the right thing to do."

Nevertheless he went. When he came to the seaside, the water was purple and dark blue and gray and dark, and not green and yellow as before. And he stood and said:

Oh, man of the sea, come listen to me,
For Alice, my wife, the plague of my life,
Has sent me to ask a boon of thee.

"Now then, what does she want?" asked the fish.

"Oh!" said the man, half-frightened. "She wants to live in a large stone castle."

"Go home. She is already standing before the door," said the fish.

Then the man went home, as he supposed. But when he arrived, there stood in the place of the cottage a great castle of stone, and his wife was standing on the steps about to go in. So she took him by the hand and said, "Let us enter."

With that he went in with her. In the castle was a great hall with a marble floor, and there were a great many servants, who led them through the large door. The passages were decked with tapestry and the rooms with golden chairs and tables. Crystal chandeliers were hanging from the ceiling, and all the rooms had carpets. The tables were spread with the most delicious foods for anyone who wanted them. At the back of the house was a stable

yard for horses and cattle and carriages of the
finest. Besides, there was a splendid large garden
with the most beautiful flowers and fine fruit
trees, and also a park, full half a mile long, with
deer, oxen, sheep, and everything the heart
could wish for.

"There," said the wife, "is not this beautiful?"

"Oh, yes," said the man. "If it will only last,
we can live in this fine castle and be very
well contented."

"We will see about that," said the wife.

The next morning the wife awakened at the
break of day, and she looked out of her window
and saw the beautiful country lying all around.

"Husband," she called, "look out of the window. Just think if we could be king over all this country. Go to your fish and tell him we should like to be king."

"Now, wife," said the man, "what should we be kings for? I don't want to be king."

"Well," said the wife, "if you don't want to be king, I will be. You must go at once to the fish. I must be king."

So the man went, very much put out that his wife should want to be king. He did not at all want to go, and yet he went all the same.

When he came to the sea, the water was dark and gray and rushed far inland, and he stood there and said:

Oh, man of the sea, come listen to me,
For Alice, my wife, the plague of my life,
Has sent me to ask a boon of thee.

"Now then, what does she want?" asked the fish.

"Oh, dear!" said the man. "She wants to be king."

"Go home. She is so already," said the fish.

So the man went back, and as he came to the palace, he saw it was very much larger and had great towers and splendid gateways. The herald stood before the door, and there were a number of soldiers with kettledrums and trumpets.

When he came inside, everything was of marble and gold, and there were many curtains with great gold tassels. Then he went through the doors to the throne room, and there was his wife, sitting upon a throne of gold and

diamonds, and she had a great golden crown on her head, and the scepter in her hand was of pure gold and jewels, and on each side stood six pages in a row, each one a head shorter than the other. So the man went up to her and said, "Well, wife, so now you are king."

"Yes," said she. "Now I am king."

Then he stood and looked at her, and when he had gazed at her for some time he said, "Well, wife, this is fine for you to be king. Now there is nothing more to ask for."

"Oh, husband!" said the wife, seeming quite restless, "I am tired of this already. Go to your fish and tell him that now I am king, I must be emperor."

"Now, wife," said the man, "what do you want to be emperor for?"

"Husband," said she, "go and tell the fish I want to be emperor."

"Oh, dear!" said the man. "He could not do it. I cannot ask him such a thing. There is but one emperor at a time. The fish can't possibly make anyone emperor—indeed he can't."

"Now, look here," said the wife, "I am king, and you are only my husband, so will you go at once? Go along. For if he was able to make me king he is able to make me emperor, and I will and must be emperor. So go along."

So he was obliged to go. And as he went he felt very uncomfortable about it, and he thought to himself, "It is not at all the right thing to do. To want to be emperor is going too far; the fish will soon get tired of this."

With this he came to the sea, and the water was quite black, and the foam flew, and the wind blew, and the man was terrified. But he stood and said:

Oh, man of the sea, come listen to me,
For Alice, my wife, the plague of my life,
Has sent me to ask a boon of thee.

"What is it now?" asked the fish.

"Oh, dear!" said the man. "My wife wants to be emperor."

"Go home," said the fish. "She is emperor already."

So the man went home and found the castle adorned with polished marble and golden gates. The troops were being marshaled before the door, and they were blowing trumpets and beating drums. And when he entered he saw barons, earls, and dukes waiting about like servants, and the doors were of bright gold. He saw his wife sitting upon a throne of solid gold, and it was about two miles high. She had a great golden crown on, set in precious stones, and in one hand she had a scepter, and in the other a globe; and on both sides of her stood pages in two rows, all arranged according to size, from the enormous giant of two miles high, to the tiniest dwarf the size of my little finger, and before her stood earls and dukes in crowds.

So the man went up to her and said, "Well, wife, so now you are emperor. I hope you are contented at last."

"We will see about that," said his wife.

···

With that they went to bed. But she was as far as ever from being contented, and she could not get to sleep for thinking of what she would like to be next.

The next morning as she sat before the window watching the sun rise, she said, "Oh, I have it! What if I should make the sun and moon to rise? Husband," she called, "wake up and go to your fish and tell him I want power over the sun and moon."

"Oh, wife!" said the man. "The fish cannot do that. Do be contented, I beg of you."

But she became most impatient and said, "I can wait no longer. Go at once."

So off he went, as well as he could for fright. And a dreadful storm arose, so that he could hardly keep on his feet. The houses and trees were blown down, and the mountains trembled, and rocks fell in the sea. The sky was quite black; and it thundered and lightninged; and the waves, crowned with foam, ran mountains high. So he cried out:

Oh, man of the sea, come listen to me,
For Alice, my wife, the plague of my life,
Has sent me to ask a boon of thee.

"Well, what now?" said the fish.

"Oh, dear!" said the man. "She wants to order about the sun and moon."

"Go home with you," said the fish, "and you will find her in the old hut."

And there they are sitting to this very day.

Ooka and
the Honest Thief

Japanese folktale
as told by I. G. Edmonds

One day, Yahichi, owner
of a rice store, came to
Ooka's court, complaining
that each night some of his
rice disappeared.

"It is such a small amount that I hesitate to
trouble your Honorable Honor," Yahichi said,
touching the ground with his head to show
proper respect for the great magistrate. "But I am
reminded of the story of the mountain that was
reduced to a plain because a single grain was
stolen from it each day for centuries."

Ooka nodded gravely. "It is just as dishonest to steal one grain of rice as it is to steal a large sack," he remarked. "Did you take proper steps to guard your property?"

"Yes, my lord. I stationed a guard with the rice each night, but still it disappears. I cannot understand it," the rice merchant said, pulling his white beard nervously.

"What about your guard. Can he be trusted?" Ooka asked.

"Absolutely, Lord Ooka," Yahichi said. "The guard is Chogoro. He has served my family for seventy-five years."

"Yes, I know Chogoro," Ooka said. "He is a most conscientious man. He could not be the thief. But it is possible that he falls asleep at his post. After all, he is eighty years old."

"A man can be just as alert at eighty as at twenty," Yahichi replied quickly. "I am eighty-one myself, and I have never been so alert. Besides, I stood guard myself with Chogoro these last two nights. The rice vanished just the same."

"In that case I will watch with you tonight," Ooka said. "I should like to see this for myself."

As he had promised, Ooka made his way that evening to Yahichi's rice store. He was sure that both Yahichi and Chogoro had fallen asleep and had allowed the thief to enter each time the rice had been stolen, and it was not long before his suspicions were proved correct. Within an hour, both men were sleeping soundly. Ooka smiled. He was certain that when the men awoke neither would admit he had slept at all.

A little past midnight, Ooka heard a slight sound outside the building. He sprang to his feet and peered cautiously out the window. To his astonishment, Ooka found himself staring straight into the face of a man standing in the shadows just outside the building. The judge recognized him as Gonta, a laborer who had been out of work for some time. The man was rooted to the spot by fear.

Ooka hesitated to arrest him. After all, he had not entered the rice store. Ooka would have no proof that he had come to steal. He could simply say that he had lost his way in the dark.

Though Ooka had recognized the thief, Gonta had not recognized the judge, for the darkness inside the building hid his face.

Ooka decided the best thing to do would be to pretend that he, too, was a thief. In this way he might trap Gonta into completing his crime. Speaking in a harsh tone to disguise his voice, he said, "You have obviously come here to steal rice just as I have."

Gonta was relieved to find himself face to face with another thief instead of a guard.

"As a favor from one thief to another," Ooka continued, "I will pass the rice out to you, so that you will not need to risk coming in yourself."

Gonta thanked him profusely for his courtesy, and Ooka picked up a large sack of rice and handed it out to him.

"This is too much," Gonta protested. "I want only a few handfuls."

Ooka was amazed. "But if you are going to steal, you may as well take a large amount. After all, if Ooka catches you, you will be punished as much for stealing a single grain as you would for a whole sack."

"That would be dishonest!" Gonta replied indignantly. "I take just enough to feed my family for a single day, for each day I hope I will find work and not have to steal anymore. If I do find work, I intend to return all I have taken."

Then he took out the amount of rice he needed for his family's daily meal and handed the sack back to the astonished judge. Thanking Ooka once more for his courtesy, Gonta turned and disappeared into the darkness. Ooka did not try to stop him.

When the shopkeeper and his guard awoke, Ooka told them what had happened.

"But why did you let the thief go?" Yahichi asked indignantly.

"Gonta is certainly a thief," Ooka replied. "But I am convinced he is an honest one, for he refused to steal more than he needed."

"But, Lord Ooka, how can a man be a thief and honest at the same time?"

"I would never have believed it possible, but it is so," Ooka said. "It is the duty of a judge to punish wickedness and reward virtue. In this case, we find both qualities in the same man, so obviously it would be unfair to treat him as any ordinary thief."

···

"But, Lord Ooka—"

"I have made my decision. Tomorrow I
will see that work is found for Gonta which is
sufficient to feed his family and still leave
enough to allow him to pay back the rice he
stole. We will see if he keeps his promise.
If he returns here and replaces the extra amount
each night, it will prove my belief that he is
an honest thief."

The plan was carried out according to Ooka's
wishes. Gonta was given a job, without knowing
that Ooka was responsible. And, as the judge
suspected, every night Gonta took the rice
left over from his day's earnings and left it in
the rice shop.

Ooka put all kinds of obstacles in his way to
make it difficult for him to enter the shop,
but this did not prevent Gonta from returning
each night, although he became more and
more afraid of being caught.

Yahichi admitted that the thief had been
punished enough for his crime and told Ooka he
did not wish to press charges. The great judge
smiled and wrote out a small scroll which he

ordered Yahichi to leave for Gonta to see when he came to pay for the last portion of rice.

When the honest thief slipped fearfully into the rice shop for the last time, he was shocked to find the scroll on which was written in Ooka's own handwriting, and bearing Ooka's signature, the following message:

You owe an extra ten percent for interest.
Honesty is the best policy.

IT'S ALL THE FAULT OF ADAM

Nigerian folktale
as told by Barbara Walker

Long ago and far away there was a poor woodcutter named Iyapò. This Iyapò lived in the smallest hut of his village, and if he had been lazy he would have gone hungry to his mat at night.

But every morning he arose very early and went out well beyond his village to the forest. There the whole morning long he cut wood, good hard wood to make hot cooking fires. As soon as the sun shone high overhead, Iyapò loaded the wood on his shoulders and walked back along the highway and through the town gate, giving a few dry sticks to the gateman for his toll. Never mind how hungry he was. He must sell his firewood before he could buy even so much as a yam for his dinner.

"Wood! Wood!" he called as he walked up and down the winding streets. "It's all the fault of Adam. Wood! Good wood for sale!" And every day somehow he managed to sell his wood.

One day as Iyapò stopped in the market to cry, "Wood! Good wood for sale!" the *oba*, the king of the town, happened to hear him.

"Who is that man?" the king asked the *otun*, his chief adviser. "And what does he mean by saying, 'It's all the fault of Adam'?"

The *otun* asked the *osi*, and the *osi* asked the *balogun*, but none of the king's officers could answer the questions.

"Go, then," said the king to the *otun*, "and bring the woodcutter to me. If he has been unjustly treated, I must know about it."

As soon as Iyapò entered, he prostrated himself, laying first his right cheek and then his left cheek on the floor of the piazza where the king sat.

"Well," said the king, "I am curious. What is your name?"

"Sire," replied the woodcutter, shaking with dread, "my name is Iyapò."

"Iyapò . . ." the king murmured into the *Irù kèrè*. "Your name means 'many troubles.' But why must you blame *Adam* for your misfortunes?"

"S-sire," stammered Iyapò, "I have heard of Adam, who long ago disobeyed God and ate a certain fruit in the Garden of Eden. If Adam had not disobeyed, we would all be happy in the Garden. And I would not have to work so hard now to earn my daily food."

"Hmmn," said the king, looking long at the
thin, ragged woodcutter. "You work hard,
and you have but little. Surely it is unfair that
someone else's disobedience should cause you
so much grief. Something must be done for you.

"Otun," the king continued, "have Iyapò
washed and dressed in clean, new clothes. Find
a room somewhere in my palace where he
can live. And take away his ragged clothes and
his bundle of wood. From now on, he will
lead a new and happy life."

Then, turning to the woodcutter, the king
nodded. "From this day forward," he said, "you
may call yourself my brother. Everything that
I have you may share. You can do anything you
want, except"—and he looked directly into
Iyapò's eyes—"*except* open the green door near
the end of the hall. That door you must never
open."

"Oh, sire," answered Iyapò joyfully, "why
should I want to open the green door? You have
already given me everything I could want
or need. I have food and clothing and shelter.
Surely I should be contented!"

For many weeks the woodcutter enjoyed his
good fortune. He ate three meals a day, instead

of one. Indeed, he ate so well that he became fat. He wore the fine new clothes the king had given him. When he tired of these, the king's servants provided him with robes even more handsomely embroidered.

Day after day, week after week, he amused himself in the king's palace, until he had quite forgotten how it felt to arise early in the morning to cut wood. He no longer remembered the pain of hunger, or the sting of disappointment. He had almost forgotten that he had ever been anything else but the king's brother.

One day as he strolled through the palace, he chanced to notice the green door. "Ah," he murmured, "that is the door I must not open. How curious! I wonder what lies behind it?" But he knew he must not open it, so he turned his back upon it.

Day by day, however, he stopped often and oftener before the green door. Without his seeming to choose that hallway himself, his feet led him there, and he wondered more and more about what lay behind the door. Each time he came closer to putting his hand upon the latch, but still he hesitated.

Then one day the king was called to another part of the town on business. "Iyapò, my brother," he said, "look after the palace in my absence. I may not be back until well past dinnertime."

"Look after the palace," Iyapò murmured as the king left the compound. "If I am to look after the palace, surely I am responsible for the room behind the green door. After all, I am the king's brother. Why should *any* room be forbidden to me?" Looking carefully here and there to be sure he was not watched, Iyapò went quietly to the green door. He listened, with his ear pressed against the door. There was not a sound from the other side. "I'll open it just a little bit," he decided, "and then I'll close it tightly again. The king will never know. But I *must* discover what is inside."

Lifting the latch, he peered into the room. He blinked and looked again. There was nothing at all in the room except his own ragged clothes and his bundle of wood! As he stood there, disbelieving, a small gray mouse hiding in a shadow in the far corner suddenly ran between Iyapò's feet and out into the hallway. "Ah!" exclaimed Iyapò. "It must be the *mouse* that the king is so careful about! I must catch him and put him back, or the king will know that I have opened the green door." Hastily latching the door, he set out after the mouse.

Up one hallway and down another raced Iyapò, with the mouse in sight but just beyond his reach. Soon he began to huff and puff. All those weeks of good eating had made him too fat to run easily. And he stumbled again and again on the wide skirt of the handsome robe he was wearing. Pausing a moment, he took off the robe and flung it on a bench. Then he ran

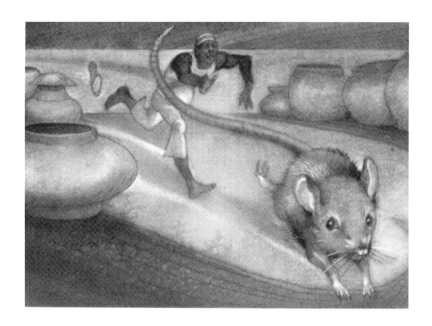

again, faster, losing his right shoe here, his left shoe there. *Still* he could not catch the little gray mouse.

"What are you doing?" The voice of the king rang through the hall.

Iyapò stopped running. His heart pounded till it seemed as if the very walls must hear it. The king! But he was not to return until well past dinnertime. . . . Suddenly Iyapò knew fear. He fell to his knees before the king.

"Oh, sire," he began, "I am sorry about your mouse."

"My *mouse*?" the king asked, puzzled. "I have no mouse. And what are you doing, running through the palace without your robe, without your shoes? The brother of the king must walk proudly, with dignity."

"You—you see, my brother," Iyapò stammered, "the mouse ran out when I opened the green door, and I knew that—"

"The green door!" exclaimed the king. "So you opened the green door. Was that not the *one thing* I told you that you must not do?"

"Oh, yes, sire, it *was*," Iyapò agreed. "And I wasn't going to open it. But day after day it was there, and day after day I wondered about it. And as the king's brother—"

"As the king's brother," the king interrupted, his eyes blazing with anger, "you felt you must be the king himself. And you thought *Adam* was disobedient! What *he* did should have taught you caution."

Iyapò prostrated himself before the king, right cheek on the floor, left cheek on the floor. Then, "What is your will, O king?" he whispered.

"Go to the green door," said the king, his voice low now, and sorrowful. "Take your ragged clothes and your bundle of wood. It is not other people's good wishes which can make you happy, but your own destiny. Sell your wood, since work is the cure for poverty. But know this, my friend: your misfortune is not the fault of Adam."

Iyapò arose. He walked on his bare feet past the fine shoes he had lost, past the handsome robe he had flung aside, to the green door. Opening it, he put on his ragged clothes, which scarcely covered his stout figure. Lifting the bundle of wood to his shoulders, he walked out of the cool palace into the dust and heat of the market. "Wood! Wood for sale!" he called. "Wood! Good wood for sale!" But no matter how many times he cried his "Wood for sale!" there was no longer a mention of Adam.

He heard a voice crying out from the shadows.

THE MONSTER
WHO GREW SMALL

Joan Grant

Far to the South, beyond the Third Cataract,
there was a small village where a certain boy
lived with his uncle. The uncle was known
as the Brave One because he was a hunter and
killed such a lot of large animals, and he was
very horrid to his nephew because he thought
the boy was a coward. He tried to frighten him
by telling stories of the terrible monsters that
he said lived in the forest, and the boy believed
what he was told, for was not his uncle called
the Brave One, the Mighty Hunter?

Whenever the boy had to go down to the river he thought that crocodiles would eat him, and when he went into the forest he thought that the shadows concealed snakes and that hairy spiders waited under the leaves to pounce on him. The place that always felt especially dangerous was on the path down to the village, and whenever he had to go along it he used to run.

One day, when he came to the most frightening part of this path, he heard a voice crying out from the shadows of the darkest trees. He put his fingers in his ears and ran even faster, but he could still hear the voice. His fear was very loud, but even so he could hear his heart, and it said to him:

"Perhaps the owner of that voice is much more frightened than you are. You know what it feels like to be frightened. Don't you think you ought to help?"

So he took his fingers out of his ears, and clenched his fists to make himself feel braver, and plunged into the deep shade, thrusting his

way between
thorn trees in the
direction of the cries.

He found a Hare caught by the leg in a tangle
of creepers, and the Hare said to him, "I was
so very frightened, but now you have come I am
not afraid anymore. You must be very brave to
come alone into the forest."

The boy released the Hare and quieted it
between his hands, saying, "I am not at all brave.
In my village they call me Miobi, the Frightened
One. I should never have dared to come here,
only I heard you calling."

The Hare said to him, "Why are you
frightened? What are you frightened of?"

"I am frightened of the crocodiles who live in
the river and of the snakes and the spiders that
lie in wait for me whenever I go out. But most of
all I am frightened of the Things which rustle
in the palm thatch over my bed place—my uncle
says they are only rats and lizards, but I know
they are far worse than that."

"What you want," said the Hare, "is a house
with walls three cubits thick, where you could
shut yourself away from all the things you fear."

"I don't think that would do any good," said
Miobi. "For if there were no windows I should
be afraid of not being able to breathe, and if

70

there *were* windows I should always be watching them, waiting for Things to creep in to devour me."

The Hare seemed to have stopped being frightened, and Miobi said to it, "Now that you know that I am not at all brave, I don't suppose I'll seem much of a protection. But if you feel I'd be better than nothing I'll carry you home, if you'll tell me where you live."

To Miobi's astonishment, the Hare replied, "I live in the Moon, so you can't come home with me, yet. But I should like to give you something to show how grateful I am for your kindness. What would you like to have best in the world?"

"I should like to have Courage . . . but I suppose that's one of the things which can't be given."

"I can't *give* it to you, but I can tell you where to find it. The road which leads there you will have to follow alone. But when your fears are strongest, look up to the Moon and I will tell you how to overcome them."

Then the Hare told Miobi about the road he must follow, and the next morning, before his uncle was awake, the boy set out on his journey.

His only weapon was a dagger that the Hare had given him. It was long and keen, pale as moonlight.

Soon the road came to a wide river. Then Miobi was very frightened, for in it there floated many crocodiles, who watched him with their evil little eyes. But he remembered what the Hare had told him, and after looking up to the Moon, he shouted at them:

"If you want to be killed come and attack me!"

Then he plunged into the river, his dagger clutched in his hand, and began to swim to the far bank.

72

Much to the crocodiles' surprise, they found
themselves afraid of him. To try to keep up their
dignity, they said to each other, "He is too thin to
be worth the trouble of eating!" And they shut
their eyes and pretended not to notice him.
So Miobi crossed the river safely and went on
his way.

After a few more days he saw two snakes,
each so large that it could have swallowed an ox
without getting a pain. Both speaking at the
same time, they said loudly, "If you come one
step further we shall immediately eat you."

Miobi was very frightened, for snakes were
one of the things he minded most. He was
on the point of running away when he looked
up to the Moon, and immediately he knew
what the Hare wanted him to do.

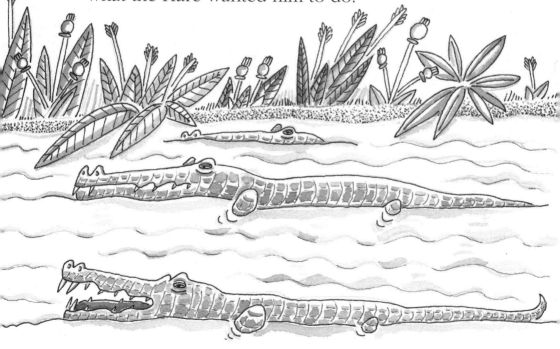

"O Large and Intelligent Serpents," he said politely, "a boy so small as myself could do no more than give *one* of you a satisfactory meal. Half of me would not be worth the trouble of digesting. Hadn't you better decide between yourselves by whom I am to have the honor of being eaten?"

"Sensible, very. I will eat you myself," said the first serpent.

"No you won't, he's mine," said the second.

"Nonsense, you had that rich merchant. He was so busy looking after his gold that he never noticed you until you got him by the legs."

"Well, what about the woman who was admiring her face in a mirror? You said she was the tenderest meal you'd had for months."

"The merchant was *since* that," said the first serpent firmly.

"He wasn't."

"He was."

"Wasn't!"

"Was!!"

While the serpents were busy arguing which of them should eat Miobi, he had slipped past without their noticing and was already out of sight. So that morning neither of the serpents had even a small breakfast.

Miobi felt so cheerful that he began to whistle. For the first time, he found himself enjoying the shapes of trees and the colors of flowers instead of wondering what dangers they might be concealing.

Soon he came in sight of a village, and even in the distance he could hear a sound of lamentation. As he walked down the single street no one took any notice of him, for the people were too busy moaning and wailing. The cooking fires were unlit, and goats were bleating because no one had remembered to milk them. Babies were crying because they were hungry, and a small girl was yelling because she had fallen down and cut her knee and her mother wasn't even interested. Miobi went to the house of the Headman, whom he found sitting cross-legged, with ashes on his head, his eyes shut, and his fingers in his ears.

Miobi had to shout very loud to make him hear. Then the old man opened one ear and one eye and growled, "What do you want?"

"Nothing," said Miobi politely. "I wanted to ask what *you* wanted. Why is your village so unhappy?"

"You'd be unhappy," said the Headman crossly, "if you were going to be eaten by a Monster."

"Who is going to be eaten? You?"

"Me and everyone else, even the goats. Can't you hear them bleating?"

Miobi was too polite to suggest that the goats were only bleating because no one had milked them. So he asked the Headman, "There seem to be quite a lot of people in your village. Couldn't you kill the Monster if you all helped?"

"Impossible!" said the Headman. "Too big, too fierce, too terrible. We are *all* agreed on that."

"What does the Monster look like?" asked Miobi.

"They say it has the head of a crocodile and the body of a hippopotamus and a tail like a very fat snake, but it's sure to be even worse. Don't talk about it!" He put his hands over his face and rocked backwards and forwards, moaning to himself.

"If you will tell me where the Monster lives, I will try to kill it for you," said Miobi, much to his own surprise.

"Perhaps you are wise," said the Headman, "for then you will be eaten first and won't have so long to think about it. The Monster lives in the cave on the top of that mountain. The smoke you can see comes from his fiery breath, so you'll be cooked before you are eaten."

Miobi looked up to the Moon and he knew what the Hare wanted him to say, so he said it:

"I will go up to the mountain and challenge the Monster."

Climbing the mountain took him a long time, but when he was halfway up he could see the Monster quite clearly. Basking at the mouth of its cave, its fiery breath wooshing out of its nostrils, it looked about three times as big as the Royal Barge—which is very big, even for a monster.

Miobi said to himself, "I won't look at it again until I have climbed all the distance between me and the cave. Otherwise I might feel too much like running away to be able to go on climbing."

When next he looked at the Monster he expected it to be much larger than it had seemed from farther away. But instead it looked quite definitely smaller, only a little bigger than one Royal Barge instead of three. The Monster saw him. It snorted angrily, and the snort flared down the mountainside and scorched Miobi. He ran back rather a long way before he could make himself stop. Now the Monster seemed to have grown larger again. It was *quite* three times as large as the Royal Barge—perhaps four.

Miobi said to himself, "This is very curious indeed. The farther I run away from the Monster, the larger it seems, and the nearer I am to it, the smaller it seems. Perhaps if I was *very* close it might be a reasonable size for me to kill with my dagger."

So that he would not be blinded by the fiery breath, he shut his eyes. And so that he would not drop his dagger, he clasped it very tightly. And so that he would not have time to start being frightened, he ran as fast as he could up the mountain to the cave.

When he opened his eyes he couldn't see anything which needed killing. The cave seemed empty, and he began to think that he must have run in the wrong direction. Then he felt something hot touch his right foot. He looked down, and there was the Monster— and it was as small as a frog! He picked it up in his hand and scratched its back. It was no more than comfortably warm to hold, and it made a small, friendly sound, halfway between a purr and the simmer of a cooking pot.

Miobi thought, "Poor little Monster! It will feel so lonely in this enormous cave." Then he thought, "It might make a nice pet, and its fiery breath would come in useful for lighting my cooking fire." So he carried it carefully down the mountain, and it curled up in his hand and went to sleep.

When the villagers saw Miobi, at first they thought they must be dreaming, for they had been so sure the Monster would kill him. Then they acclaimed him as a hero, saying, "Honor to the mighty hunter! He, the bravest of all! He, who has slain the Monster!"

Miobi felt very embarrassed, and as soon as he could make himself heard above the cheering, he said, "But I didn't kill it. I brought it home as a pet."

They thought that was only the modesty becoming to a hero, and before they would believe him he had to explain how the Monster had only seemed big so long as he was running away, and that the nearer he got to it the smaller it grew, until at last, when he was standing beside it, he could pick it up in his hand.

The people crowded round to see the Monster.
It woke up, yawned a small puff of smoke,
and began to purr. A little girl said to Miobi,
"What is its name?"

"I don't know," said Miobi, "I never asked it."

It was the Monster himself who answered her
question. He stopped purring, looked round to
make sure everyone was listening, and then said:

"I have many names. Some call me Famine,
and some Pestilence, but the most pitiable
of humans give me their own names." It yawned
again, and then added, "But most people
call me What-Might-Happen."

In wonder and delight, he saw three beautiful girls.

The Selkie Girl

Scottish folktale
as told by Susan Cooper

The islands rise green out of the sea, where the waves foam over the gray rocks, and strange things may happen there.

Donallan lived on the biggest island. He had a small farmhouse called a croft, with ten sheep grazing a few acres of land, and he had a boat for fishing in the sea. His parents were dead and he had no wife, so he lived there, with only a dog called Angus, to herd the sheep, and a cat called Cat, to keep the croft free of mice. He was lonely sometimes. He would listen to the wind singing in the chimney and wish it were a human voice.

One spring morning, Donallan went down to the beach, with his dog Angus for company, to rake up the seaweed that he dug into his garden each year. He had gathered a great bale of weed when he thought he heard music from the rocks beside the sea. It was like the voice of the wind, but Donallan was a long way from his chimney. He went to look, and in wonder and delight, he saw three beautiful girls sitting on the rocks, naked, combing their long hair.

One of the girls had fair hair, one red, and one black. The fair-haired girl was singing. She was the most beautiful of the three, and Donallan could not take his eyes from her. He gazed and gazed at her gleaming white body and her long-lashed dark eyes, and he listened to her lilting voice singing its wordless song. And he knew suddenly that he would never be happy unless he could share his life with this magical girl.

Then Angus the dog turned from chasing a crab and saw the girls, and he began to growl deep in his throat, like summer thunder far away. The three girls looked up, startled, and saw Donallan and his dog. In an instant, each of them

snatched up a shapeless bundle that was lying at her side and plunged over the edge of the rocks into the sea. And all at once they were no longer girls but selkies, gray seals, three sleek shapes flashing dark through the waves.

Donallan stood on the beach, forlorn. "Come back!" he called to his memory of the lovely singing girl. "Oh, come back!"

But nothing was there but the empty sea.

Donallan went sadly home, carrying his bale of seaweed, and on the way he met Old Thomas. Thomas was the most ancient man in the islands; he had a lame leg and only three teeth left in his head, but he had sharp eyes. "And what is the matter with you, Donallan?" he said. "Did the sea take your boat in exchange for that fine weed?"

Donallan sighed. "I am in love," he said, and he told Old Thomas about the beautiful vanished girls who had turned into seals.

"Oh dear me," said Old Thomas, whistling through his three teeth. "A bad choice you have made. For those are the daughters of the King of Lochlann, out beyond the sea's brim, and they are selkies indeed. Just once a year, on the seventh day of the highest tides of spring, they get the land longing on them, and they slip out of their skins and take human form for a day."

"I love her, the fair-haired one," Donallan said. "I want her to be my wife."

"There's only one way for that," Old Thomas said.

"What is it then?" said Donallan quickly. "Tell me, tell me!"

Old Thomas looked thoughtfully at Donallan's bale of seaweed. "And what will you give me if I tell you?" he said.

"This fine weed for your garden," Donallan said. "And one like it every year."

"Will you carry it to my croft?"

"I will," Donallan said eagerly.

"And will you dig it into the soil?"

"I will, I will!" Donallan snatched Old Thomas up from the ground, perched him on top of the seaweed, and carried him off toward his croft. *"Tell me!"* he said.

Old Thomas grinned down at him. "You must wait until this same day next year," he said, "at the seventh stream of the flood tide in spring. And if then you are still foolish enough to be in love, you must go to that rock and steal the bundle that is beside the selkie girl, when she is out of the sea.

For that is her skin, and without it, she cannot become a seal again. You must not destroy it, or she will die; but as long as you keep it safe and hidden, she will follow you and stay with you."

Donallan shouted for joy.

Old Thomas said quietly, "But a wild creature will always go back to the wild, in the end."

Donallan paid no heed to that. He waited for a year, then went back to the rocky beach on the seventh day of the spring flood tides. There were the three girls again, the fair-haired one singing even more bewitchingly than before. Donallan crept up to the rock where they sat. The dark-haired girl caught sight of him and cried out in warning, and all three girls dived at once into the sea—but Donallan had hold of the bundled sealskin of the girl he loved.

She begged him from the waves, "Oh please, give me back my skin!"

Out in the ocean swells, Donallan could see two gleaming shapes swimming, waiting for her: a dark gray seal and one with a reddish skin.

"Come with me!" he called to the selkie girl. "Come with me and be my wife, and I will work for you and love you well, and we shall be happy all our days!" He walked away up the beach with her skin, knowing she must follow, and when she came after him, he gave her a soft woollen shawl that had belonged to his mother, to cover her nakedness. She was crying bitterly, but she followed him.

So Donallan married the selkie girl, and they lived together in the croft with the dog and the cat and the sheep outside grazing the hills. She would not tell him her true name, so he called her Mairi. He kept her sealskin hidden, checking it often to make sure it never cracked or dried out. After the first day, she never asked for it again.

Mairi worked as hard as Donallan on the croft, and because he was gentle and loving, she no longer wept. When their first child was born, he saw her smile. But he never heard her sing again, and each year when the seventh day of the flood tides came round in the spring, he would find her looking sadly out at the sea, with her head tilted as if she were listening.

As the years passed, five children were born to Mairi and Donallan: three boys and two girls. They were called Dougal, Margaret, Niall, Kate Annie, and James. They were bright, handsome children, sweet voiced and strong backed, and they lived happily on the croft by the sea. Only Kate Annie, who was thoughtful, wondered why she felt sometimes that her quiet mother had lost something precious, and wished that she could give it back to her again.

One summer day, Donallan got up very early before the sunrise because it was his day for checking secretly that the sealskin was safe and well. Softly he went outside and he pulled three stones from the wall of the house, which was as thick as a man's arm is long. Then he took out the sealskin, spread it flat on the ground, rubbed it carefully with oil, and put it back again. He did not see his youngest son, James, who had come creeping out of the house after him. James stared. What was his father doing, so secret, so early in the morning? He slipped back indoors to

his bed wondering, what was so special about the skin of a seal?

Later that day, Donallan took the three biggest children out to the fields. James went outside the house and looked at the wall. He could see the place where his father had moved the stones. He went back to his mother, who was making oatcakes with Kate Annie.

"Mother," he said, "why is my father keeping an old sealskin in our wall?"

Mairi stopped mixing the dough. Very slowly she put down the bowl and spoon on the table, and she looked at James as if she had never seen him before. Both children saw a glow of happiness like sunlight in her face, and for the first time in their lives, they heard her laugh.

"Oh, James!" she said. "You have found my skin!"

She took his hand and Kate Annie's, and the three of them ran outside and took the sealskin from the wall. Mairi laughed again in delight, and Kate Annie felt warm at the sound.

"Come," Mairi said to them, and with the skin in her arms, she led them down to the sea. Kate Annie felt frightened, and yet she knew that something right was happening, whatever it might be.

...

Their mother said to them, "Be brave, because I must leave you. For I was brought here from my own people against my will, twenty years past, and I have five children in the sea and five on the land. And that is a hard case to be in."

Kate Annie said, "We have brothers and sisters in the sea?"

"You have," she said, "and so do I."

"Don't go," James said. He blinked hard, because he felt he was too old to cry.

"I love you," Mairi said, and she stroked his hair. "I shall never be far away." She raised her head and looked out at the sea.

"You must go to them. It's their turn," Kate Annie said. She took her brother's hand. "I'll look after James."

Mairi stepped into the sea, and smiled at the wash of the waves about her feet. She said, "I shall always be here, watching over you, whether you are in the islands or on the sea. I promise you. And every year, at the seventh stream of the flood tide in spring, you will all see me as I am now."

She kissed them and she dived into the sea, holding the sealskin. Out in the ocean swells, they saw two gleaming shapes swimming, waiting for her: a dark gray seal and one with a reddish skin. Then suddenly there were three, as a light-colored seal joined them. The three curved and swirled and dived together in the foaming water—and then they were gone.

"She isn't drowned, is she?" James said.

"Of course not," said Kate Annie. "Come home and we'll bake the oatcakes."

They told Donallan, when he came back. He said sorrowfully, "Old Thomas was right, in the end." But none of the children understood what he meant.

Whenever Donallan and his children went fishing, in all the years afterward, their nets took three times as many fish as those of anyone else. When storms churned the waves and threw wrecks on the shore, their boat was always safe; there were tales that great gray seals had been seen carrying it on their backs. In spring, at the flood tide, the family would go down to the rocks by the sea, and they would come back with a look on their faces like sunlight. And still today, if you listen to the wind blowing round Donallan's house, there is a singing in it that seems to come from the sea.

"You can trust me."

THE MUSHROOM MAN

Ethel Pochocki

There once was a man who spent his days in the dark. He worked in a mushroom farm, a long, low, windowless building where mushrooms grew in beds of black soil, and everything had the earthy smell of mold.

The man rarely saw the sun, except in the summer when it rose with him, or when it streaked scarlet-purple across the sky as he walked home after work.

When the people of the town saw him on the street, they snickered at his strange appearance. They called him the mushroom man, for indeed he did resemble the crop he tended. His round, oversized head was a bit too large for the rest of his body, and his flesh, pale as paste, was spongy to the touch. His deeply set eyes blinked often, and he walked slightly bent over, with soft shuffling steps.

Children would follow him, at a safe distance, and chant in their high singsong voices:

Watch out for the mushroom man,
The mushroom man, the mushroom man,
He'll eat you up in a frying pan,
Fast as he can, fast as he can!

Then their parents would call to them and tell them to stop that right now and come home, and they would run off laughing.

The mushroom man never answered them. He just kept on walking as if he did not hear. He knew he could not change their minds. They had already judged him by his appearance. They seemed to fear that they, too, might turn into mushroom people if they got too close to him.

The mushroom man accepted this without resentment, for he had been blessed with a cheerful disposition.

For the most part, he was quite content. Still there was this little ache now and then, sometimes dull, as in old bones on a rainy day, sometimes sharp as a wasp sting. Sometimes it came when he was most content, because he had no one with whom to share his good feelings.

He knew the ache was loneliness, and he learned to live with it, as one would with a grouchy relative. "After all," he said to himself, "nothing's perfect."

He was comfortable living in the little basement room of an apartment house. When

he got home, he would open a can of vegetable soup and a box of crackers and eat his dinner in the big brown overstuffed chair that made him itch, and he would listen to the news on the radio or the ticking of his wind-up clock.

Sometimes when the weather allowed, he would make a sandwich, stick it into his pocket, and go down to the riverbank in the park. There he would sit on a bench and eat his peanut butter and marshmallow fluff sandwich, watching the strolling people and playful squirrels.

He found comfort in the antics of the squirrels. They chattered in front of him without fear. He would sometimes offer them bits of his sandwich, which they would politely decline.

As he watched them, an idea began to grow in his mind. Perhaps he might share his life with a pet. A pet would be his friend, one who would like him just as he was. He knew it would not be a squirrel—they were too nervous to listen to poetry—or a dog. He did not like dogs. He supposed there might be some good ones somewhere, but he had been chased by too many whose snarling teeth had nearly nabbed him. No, it would not be a dog.

•••

Suddenly the squirrels scurried, as a cat walked up the path toward the mushroom man. A creamy white creature with a superior air, she ambled past, ignoring him, then stopped to nab a flea on her rump. After disposing of it, she sat in the middle of the path, cleaning her ears as if it were her private dressing room.

The mushroom man could not take his eyes off her. What a delightful creature! What exquisite coloring!

The cat looked straight at him, walked over, jumped into his lap, and put her paws on his chest. He noticed that she was slightly cross-eyed, but that only added to her charm.

He stroked her white fur and rubbed her ears.

"Do you have a home, pretty one?" he asked.

"No," she purred.

"Would you like to come with me? I have sardines in the can."

"Yes," she purred even louder and licked his nose.

And so they left the park together and returned to his apartment. That night, as he settled into bed, the cat hugging his feet, he thought, "Now I am a completely happy man!"

He named the cat Beatrice, and she became absolute mistress of his home. While he worked, he thought of little else but coming home and spending the evening with Beatrice, watching her enchanting tricks and listening to her vast collection of songs.

Beatrice enjoyed the attention, the adoration, the chicken livers, the satin pillow—but after a while, she grew weary of it. Oh, the man was kind in a dull sort of way, but she was beginning to tire of being locked up and treated like a delicate toy. At heart, she was not one who could be satisfied with hearth and home.

"I was born to wander," she sighed plaintively as she sat before the mirror, pluming her tail like a peacock. She decided it would be best for both of them if she left before the mushroom man became too attached.

And so one starry night as they sat on the bench in the park and he began explaining to her the position of Venus in the autumn sky, she quietly disappeared into a clump of yew bushes.

The mushroom man searched, calling out to her, pleading for her return, but Beatrice never came back. He sat on the bench, sighing sadly. Perhaps it was his fate to be alone.

The earth beneath his feet began to move. Something was making a tunnel. Then more

tunnels spread out, crisscrossing each other like sled tracks in the snow. The plowing stopped. A small black-furred animal with a long, narrow nose burst from a tunnel and appeared to be checking out his workmanship.

"Helloo—" said the mushroom man softly, so as not to startle the creature. The animal dashed back into the hole, almost missing it in his panic.

"Please come back," cried the man, "I won't hurt you! We could enjoy the evening together. I just want to be friendly."

After a short silence, a muffled response came from the tunnel. "We can talk, but I'll stay down here, thank you."

•••

"Oh, please come out," pleaded the mushroom man, "whoever you are! It's such a lovely night. Don't you love the moonlight? I much prefer it to the sun."

A furry head appeared, slowly, cautiously. "I'm a mole, and I'll stay right here, thank you. You have a kind voice, but I can't afford to go around trusting anyone. You could be waiting to trick me with a trap or poison."

"You can trust *me*," said the mushroom man. "I said I won't hurt you, and I'm a man of my word. You can sit over there by that clump of irises. I couldn't reach you if I tried. Come, share the moonlight."

"Don't you know anything about moles?" asked the animal in weary exasperation. "Moles are blind. We can't see the moonlight or irises or anything."

"Oh, I *am* sorry," said the mushroom man, embarrassed. "I didn't realize—please forgive me."

The mole emerged from the hole completely. "Nothing to forgive," he said a bit too cheerfully. "That's just the way things are, and we do quite well, thank you, without sight. No point in making a fuss."

"I admire your spunk and courage," said the mushroom man.

"Well," said the mole, his voice quivering slightly, "I can stand being in the dark, but it's being alone that's difficult. I lost most of my family in a flood—I escaped when I was thrown headfirst into a drainpipe. The others were caught in a trap and made into a muff."

"I'm so sorry," the mushroom man said again. "I—I am quite alone myself. As for the dark, I'm rather fond of it. I think there's much to be said for being in the dark. Would you believe that I even work in the dark all day?"

"No, go on!" said the mole, wiping away the few tears that had escaped when he spoke of his lost family.

...

The mushroom man told him about the farm and how he picked and packed the pearly beauties by the light of his headlamp.

"Do you like mushrooms?" he asked the mole.

The mole laughed, lightly at first, and then with such gusto he began to roll around in a patch of wild peppermint.

"What's so funny?" asked the mushroom man.

"*Do I like mushrooms?* My friend, mushrooms are right up there with worms and grubs! I could show you mushrooms you wouldn't believe. Right *now*—what do you say, are you up for adventure?"

"Of course!" cried the mushroom man, almost dancing at the thought of a shared adventure.

Off they went lickety-split into the deep woods. Even though he was blind, the mole was swift and sure of the path. The mushroom man could barely keep up with him. They came to an oak tree on a small hill, and the mole began to sniff and dig into the side of it. In a few moments, he came up with something dark and squishy in the shape of a flattened ear.

"Truffles!" exclaimed the mushroom man. "The rarest and most delicious of all mushrooms! I haven't had a truffle in ages. I shall cook it up with a bit of butter and a dash of wine. Will you do me the honor of sharing this delicacy?"

The mole did not answer. He remembered his unfortunate relatives made into a muff. Could he trust a human?

"It has been a long time since I have had a dinner guest," the mushroom man said softly. "We could tell riddles and write poems, and you could tell me about life beneath the earth. Do you like apple crisp?"

The mole decided to risk all. "Of course I will come. How kind of you to invite me," he said, knowing he had sealed his fate, for better or worse. And off they went, without further talk.

After dinner, which each assured the other was the most scrumptious ever, they ate yogurt-covered raisins and toasted their feet by the artificial fire. (The mole, never having seen a real fireplace, said the crackling sounded quite real to him.) They talked of many things and found they were in agreement about most of them, and then they said good night, promising to meet the next evening for dinner.

And so they did, and for every evening thereafter, until the trees were bare of leaves. With the first frost, the mushroom man invited

the mole to spend the winter with him, and the mole accepted. The mushroom man brought a basket of dirt from the mushroom farm and set it up in the cool pantry, so the mole could burrow himself a bed.

During the day, the mole tended to the house—washed the dishes, shook out the rugs, made lentil soup and banana fritters—because he was very smart and remembered where everything was.

When Christmas arrived, they trimmed a small fir tree with cranberries and dried apple rings, nibbling as they worked. The mole gave the mushroom man a pair of sunglasses with sparkly red rims, a vanilla bean, and a poem he wrote about moon shadows dancing on the snow, as he imagined them. (The mushroom man framed it the day after Christmas and hung it above the fireplace.)

The mushroom man gave the mole a tin of worms imported from France, two pairs of green wool slipper socks (one pair for the front paws, one for the back), and a music box that played "You Are My Sunshine."

Each declared his gifts exactly what he most wanted, but they agreed, as they sat before the fire sipping spiced cider, that the very best gift of all was having a friend.

She kept her studies a secret.

THE PRINCESS AND THE BEGGAR

Korean folktale as told by
Anne Sibley O'Brien

In an ancient kingdom, a craggy mountain rises
out of the mist. Peony Peak, it is called. Below,
a wide green river valley stretches down to
the sea. Nestled in the curve of the river is
the ancient walled city of Pyung-yang,
where . . . once upon a time, there
lived a king whose youngest
and favorite daughter was
known to all as the
Weeping Princess.

...

On a bright spring morning, the great wooden palace gates creaked open. "Make way! Make way for the royal family!" bellowed a herald. "The queen and her daughters travel to the Spring Pavilion!"

But as the procession reached the market at East Gate, the royal family was jostled by the boisterous crowd. "Make way! Make way for the royal family!" the herald repeated, but the market did not give way. Chickens squawked, dogs barked, hawkers bawled, buyers bickered, all at the top of their lungs.

Suddenly the bearers of the third sedan chair halted.

"Yaaah, clumsy dog! Out of the way!" the herald yelled. The youngest princess peeked out from behind the brocade flap. A filthy boy lay sprawled in the mud.

"It's only the beggar boy, Ondal!" said the herald. "Hey, Pabo! Pabo Ondal! Move out of the way!" he yelled, kicking the boy aside. The princess was too frightened to protest, but tears of sympathy welled up in her eyes.

As they alighted at the pavilion, her sister teased, "There she goes again, our Weeping Princess!"

The princess sobbed harder. Her mother sighed. "Why does she cry about everything? What man will want a wife who cries all the time?!"

115

Six summers passed. The winter snows lined the riverbanks with ice, and the northern winds were bitter. In the marketplace, vendors huddled over their fires and exchanged stories about the beggar, Ondal.

"He lives among the creatures in the mountains," said one. "No better than an animal," agreed another. In time, their wild stories reached even the ears of the king.

On the first morning of the new year, the youngest princess gathered with her sisters and brothers in the Grand Palace. But as she made her bow before the king, she tripped and stumbled. Tears silently spilled down her cheeks.

"Heh, heh! What's this noise? Who's crying on the first day of the new year?" teased the king. "Speak up! Speak up!" But when the princess remained silent, the king frowned with displeasure.

116

"This daughter is impossible! If she keeps crying at every little thing, we'll . . . marry her off to the beggar, Pabo Ondal!" His humor once more restored, the king chuckled at his joke.

The queen turned pale at his words. "Do not speak of such things on the first day of the new year," she rebuked him.

But it was too late. Everyone in court had heard the king's joke. From that moment, the Weeping Princess had no peace. There was always someone nearby to tease, "Oh, ho! You'll be the wife of Pabo Ondal! The king himself has said so!"

"Did you know he wears animal skins and sleeps in a cave?" "He tears his meat raw from the bones!"

The princess only cried harder. She hid in the palace library and consoled herself by reading her favorite poems and adventurous tales of dragons and tigers. But for fear of ridicule, she kept her studies a secret.

When the princess was in her sixteenth year, the king announced to the court, "It is time for the youngest princess to marry. I have arranged a most excellent match with the noble son of Ko."

The princess considered her future life as a noblewoman—running a household under her mother-in-law's direction, with only frivolous parties and court gossip for entertainment. No solitude, no secret studies. "I will be miserable," she thought.

"Sir . . . I cannot accept," the princess whispered.

"You *cannot*? What do you mean, you cannot?" shouted the king. "I have arranged a fine match

for which any sensible girl would be grateful!
You say you *cannot*? You *will* obey me!"
he thundered.

In desperation, the princess searched for
an excuse. "I most humbly beg your pardon,
most Honored Father . . . but before I wed
the son of noble Ko, I . . . I would be the
wife of Pabo Ondal!"

The king's
eyes bulged like
a warrior demon's,
his eyebrows
bristling. "The wife
of Pabo Ondal?!
What nonsense
is this?"

"But, Esteemed
Father," she pressed
on recklessly, "*you* said
you would marry me to
Pabo Ondal. How can the
king go back on his word?"

"Go then to your Pabo Ondal
before you bring more shame
upon your family!" Enraged beyond
reason, the king banished his
favorite daughter from the palace.

Just before dawn, the princess left the
palace alone and on foot for the first time.
She carried one small bundle, a parting
gift of gold pieces from the queen.

The princess walked in the direction of
Peony Peak, for Pabo Ondal's hut was said
to be at the foot of the mountain path.

···

At sundown, she reached a clearing where a shabby straw-roofed hut stood alone. The princess wiped away tears of exhaustion mingled with fear. She jumped at the sound of a voice, raw and grating.

"Why do you weep?"

"I have come to be the wife of Ondal," the princess whispered.

"Why do you mock me?" the voice asked harshly.

"If Ondal will not have me," the princess replied humbly, "then I have nowhere to go. I have been banished from my home."

A man with matted hair and ragged clothes stepped up from behind her. Slowly he reached out and gently brushed away her tears with his rough fingers.

That year the rains washed in summer's brilliant greens in the clearing at the foot of Peony Peak. The princess shyly followed Ondal as he gathered roots and hunted in the forest. Ondal watched as she patiently stitched fine linen garments to replace his tattered clothing. In time—as they planted, tended, and mended together, they learned not to fear each other.

In the winter, deep snows filled the mountain pass. On the long dark evenings, the princess recited her favorite poems to Ondal. She also taught him how to read and write.

The princess marveled at the quickness with which Ondal learned. She remembered his many kindnesses to her and his gentleness with the creatures of the forest. "How terrible that the village people call him a wild beast and an idiot! Those who mock him shall learn the truth," she decided.

•••

On the first warm day, the princess placed two
gold pieces in Ondal's palm. "Husband, you
must go to the market in the city and buy a
horse. The horse may be weak and lame as long
as it is of royal lineage."

Ondal was reluctant to do her bidding for
he feared the scorn of the villagers. But the
princess persuaded him. "See how we both
have changed. You are no longer Pabo Ondal
the beggar, and I am no Weeping Princess."

Ondal returned the next nightfall,
leading a scrawny, unkempt horse.

···

The princess and Ondal cared tenderly for the horse. When the horse grew strong enough, the princess began Ondal's riding lessons.

Another year passed, and spring once again came to the clearing. One morning the princess turned to Ondal. "Husband," said she, "on the third day of the third month, the king holds the Festival of the Hunters. This year, you are ready to join the hunt." Ondal protested, but once again the princess persuaded him to do her bidding.

At the king's hunting festival, a mysterious rider dressed as a commoner startled the noble huntsmen with his fearless exploits. But before they could discover his identity, he disappeared. The curious onlookers talked among themselves.

"On the Full Moon Night of the fifth month, the king will hold the Festival of the Scholars. Surely a nobleman of such talent will enter the poetry contest."

News of the competition reached even the hut at the foot of Peony Peak.

"Husband, you must compete with the scholars," the princess told Ondal. A third time,

•••

Ondal agreed to do his wife's bidding. He was overjoyed when the princess prepared to accompany him into the city.

They arrived in the capital on the afternoon of the festival. The sounds of drums and flutes and gongs filled the city streets, now crowded with masked dancers, farmers' bands, and peddlers selling spring wine and sweets to hungry spectators. Ondal and the princess wandered the festive streets until dusk.

As evening fell, Ondal joined the scholars at the Lotus Pavilion. Only he was dressed in commoner's clothing. The noblemen protested. "Everyone knows peasants neither read nor write!"

Ondal silenced them. "What then have you to fear?"

When the moon rose to brighten the darkened sky, the crowd hushed. Ondal bowed his head in contemplation. He prepared his ink. With firm strokes, he brushed the characters of his poem.

"Such simplicity!" "Such swiftness!" "Such strength!" whispered the judges in admiration.

The first judge lifted Ondal's scroll and read for all to hear:

> *On the wild mountain*
> *a lone orchid,*
> *filled with dew,*
> *trembles.*
> *The drops spill,*
> *fall on a withered seedling.*
> *The dying pine stirs to life.*

The onlookers broke into applause. Standing among them, the princess wiped a tear from the corner of her eye.

The king clapped loudest of all. He called the winner of the poetry contest before him.

"Are you not the skilled huntsman from the hunting festival?" the king demanded.

"Royal Highness," replied Ondal, "I am he."

"What of your common appearance? How is it possible that you have mastered the royal arts?" questioned the king.

"Most noble sir, all that I have learned, I owe to my esteemed wife."

"Oh, ho!" exclaimed the king. "Such a woman of talent I would like to see! Have her come forward at once!" he ordered.

The princess approached the Lotus Pavilion and stood beside Ondal. She bowed with perfect grace before the king. "Royal Highness," she said, "in earlier days my husband was known by the name of Pabo Ondal."

The news spread quickly through the crowd. "The banished princess has returned!" "The stranger is he who was called Pabo Ondal!" "A peasant has won the king's poetry contest!"

Finally the king spoke. "My daughter has returned," he proclaimed, "bringing me a new

···

son worthy of honor. You have won the king's favor. What do you ask of me?"

At Ondal's nod, the princess replied, "Honored Father. We are but simple folk. We ask only to serve when you have need."

And so it came to pass in the years that followed, Ondal's services to the king were many and great, but his happiness awaited him at the foot of Peony Peak.

The wind swept bitterly across the peak.

THE FIRE ON
THE MOUNTAIN

Ethiopian folktale as told by
Harold Courlander and Wolf Leslau

People say that in the old days in the city of Addis Ababa there was a young man by the name of Arha. He had come as a boy from the country of Guragé, and in the city he became the servant of a rich merchant, Haptom Hasei.

Haptom Hasei was so rich that he owned everything that money could buy, and often he was very bored because he had tired of everything he knew, and there was nothing new for him to do.

One cold night, when the damp wind was blowing across the plateau, Haptom called

to Arha to bring wood for the fire. When Arha was finished, Haptom began to talk.

"How much cold can a man stand?" he said, speaking at first to himself. "I wonder if it would be possible for a man to stand on the highest peak, Mount Sululta, where the coldest winds blow, through an entire night, without blankets or clothing, and yet not die?"

"I don't know," Arha said. "But wouldn't it be a foolish thing?"

"Perhaps, if he had nothing to gain by it, it would be a foolish thing to spend the night

···

that way," Haptom said. "But I would be willing to bet that a man couldn't do it."

"I am sure a courageous man could stand naked on Mount Sululta throughout an entire night and not die of it," Arha said. "But as for me, it isn't my affair since I've nothing to bet."

"Well, I'll tell you what," Haptom said. "Since you are so sure it can be done, I'll make a bet with you anyway. If you can stand among the rocks on Mount Sululta for an entire night, without food or water or clothing or blankets or fire, and not die of it, then I will give you

ten acres of good farmland for your own,
with a house and cattle."

Arha could hardly believe what he had heard.

"Do you really mean this?" he asked.

"I am a man of my word," Haptom replied.

"Then tomorrow night I will do it," Arha said,
"and afterward, for all the years to come, I shall
till my own soil."

But he was very worried, because the wind
swept bitterly across the peak. So in the morning
Arha went to a wise old man from the Guragé
tribe and told him of the bet he had made.
The old man listened quietly and thoughtfully,
and when Arha had finished he said:

"I will help you. Across the valley from Sululta
is a high rock which can be seen in the daytime.
Tomorrow night, as the sun goes down, I shall
build a fire there, so that it can be seen from
where you stand on the peak. All night long you
must watch the light of my fire. Do not close
your eyes or let the darkness creep upon you. As
you watch my fire, think of its warmth, and think
of me, your friend, sitting there tending it for
you. If you do this, you will survive, no matter
how bitter the night wind."

Arha thanked the old man warmly and went back to Haptom's house with a light heart. He told Haptom he was ready, and in the afternoon Haptom sent him, under the watchful eyes of other servants, to the top of Mount Sululta. There, as night fell, Arha removed his clothes and stood in the damp cold wind that swept across the plateau with the setting sun. Across the valley, several miles away, Arha saw the light of his friend's fire, which shone like a star in the blackness.

The wind turned colder and seemed to pass
through his flesh and chill the marrow in his
bones. The rock on which he stood felt like ice.
Each hour the cold numbed him more, until
he thought he would never be warm again, but
he kept his eyes upon the twinkling light across
the valley and remembered that his old friend
sat there tending a fire for him. Sometimes wisps
of fog passed. He sneezed and coughed and

shivered and began to feel ill. Yet all night
through he stood there, and only when the dawn
came did he put on his clothes and go down
the mountain back to Addis Ababa.

Haptom was very surprised to see Arha, and
he questioned his servants thoroughly.

"Did he stay all night without food or drink
or blankets or clothing?"

"Yes," his servants said. "He did all of these
things."

"Well, you are a strong fellow," Haptom said to Arha. "How did you manage to do it?"

"I simply watched the light of a fire on a distant hill," Arha said.

"What! You watched a fire? Then you lose the bet and you are still my servant and you own no land!"

"But this fire was not close enough to warm me, it was far across the valley!"

"I won't give you the land," Haptom said. "You didn't fulfill the conditions. It was only the fire that saved you."

Arha was very sad. He went again to his friend of the Guragé tribe and told him what had happened.

"Take the matter to the judge," the old man advised him.

Arha went to the judge and complained, and the judge sent for Haptom. When Haptom told his story, and the servants said once more that Arha had watched a distant fire across the valley, the judge said:

"No, you have lost, for Haptom Hasei's condition was that you must be without fire."

Once more Arha went to his old friend with the sad news that he was doomed to the life of a servant, as though he had not gone through the ordeal on the mountaintop.

"Don't give up hope," the old man said. "More wisdom grows wild in the hills than in any city judge."

He got up from where he sat and went to find a man named Hailu, in whose house he had been a servant when he was young.

He explained to the good man about the
bet between Haptom and Arha, and asked if
something couldn't be done.

"Don't worry about it," Hailu said after
thinking for a while. "I will take care
of it for you."

Some days later Hailu sent invitations to
many people in the city to come to a feast at his
house. Haptom was among them, and so was
the judge who had ruled Arha had lost the bet.

When the day of the feast arrived, the guests
came riding on mules with fine trappings, their
servants strung out behind them on foot. Haptom
came with twenty servants, one of whom held
a silk umbrella over his head to shade him
from the sun, and four drummers played music
that signified the great Haptom was here.

The guests sat on soft rugs laid out for them
and talked. From the kitchen came the odors
of wonderful things to eat: roast goat, roast corn
and durra, pancakes called *injera*, and many
tantalizing sauces. The smell of the food only
accentuated the hunger of the guests. Time
passed. The food should have been served,

but they didn't see it, only smelled vapors that
drifted from the kitchen. The evening came,
and still no food was served. The guests began
to whisper among themselves. It was very
curious that the honorable Hailu had not had
the food brought out. Still the smells came from
the kitchen. At last one of the guests spoke
out for all the others:

"Hailu, why do you do this to us? Why do you invite us to a feast and then serve us nothing?"

"Why, can't you smell the food?" Hailu asked with surprise.

"Indeed we can, but smelling is not eating, there is no nourishment in it!"

"And is there warmth in a fire so distant that it can hardly be seen?" Hailu asked. "If Arha was warmed by the fire he watched while standing on Mount Sululta, then you have been fed by the smells coming from my kitchen."

The people agreed with him; the judge now saw his mistake, and Haptom was shamed. He thanked Hailu for his advice, and announced that Arha was then and there the owner of the land, the house, and the cattle.

Then Hailu ordered the food brought in, and the feast began.

ACKNOWLEDGMENTS

All possible care has been taken to trace ownership and secure permission for each selection in this series. The Great Books Foundation wishes to thank the following authors, publishers, and representatives for permission to reprint copyrighted material:

THE BANZA, by Diane Wolkstein. Copyright © 1978, 1981 by Diane Wolkstein. Reprinted by permission of the author.

The Man Whose Trade Was Tricks, from YES AND NO STORIES, by George and Helen Papashvily. Copyright © 1946, 1974 by George and Helen Papashvily. Reprinted by permission of HarperCollins Publishers.

Ooka and the Honest Thief, from OOKA THE WISE: TALES OF OLD JAPAN, by I. G. Edmonds. Copyright © 1961, 1989 by I. G. Edmonds. Reprinted by permission of Barry N. Malzberg.

It's All the Fault of Adam, from THE DANCING PALM TREE AND OTHER NIGERIAN FOLKTALES, by Barbara Walker. Copyright © 1968 by Barbara Walker. Reprinted by permission of Texas Tech University Press for Barbara Walker, holder of all text rights.

THE SELKIE GIRL, by Susan Cooper. Copyright © 1986 by Susan Cooper. Reprinted by permission of Margaret K. McElderry Books, an imprint of Simon & Schuster Children's Publishing Division.

THE MUSHROOM MAN, by Ethel Pochocki. Copyright © 1993 by Ethel Pochocki. Reprinted by permission of the author.

THE PRINCESS AND THE BEGGAR, by Anne Sibley O'Brien. Copyright © 1993 by Anne Sibley O'Brien. Reprinted by permission of Scholastic Inc.

The Fire on the Mountain, from THE FIRE ON THE MOUNTAIN AND OTHER STORIES FROM ETHIOPIA AND ERITREA, by Harold Courlander and Wolf Leslau. Copyright © 1978 by Harold Courlander and Wolf Leslau. Reprinted by permission of the Emma Courlander Trust.

ILLUSTRATION CREDITS

Leo and Diane Dillon prepared the illustrations for *Ooka and the Honest Thief* and for *The Fire on the Mountain*.

Tom Feelings prepared the illustrations for *It's All the Fault of Adam*. Reprinted by permission of the Estate of Tom Feelings.

Wanda Gág's illustrations for *The Fisherman and His Wife* are from TALES FROM GRIMM, by Jacob and Wilhelm Grimm, freely translated and illustrated by Wanda Gág. Copyright © 1936 by Wanda Gág; renewed 1964 by Robert Janssen. Reprinted by permission of the Wanda Gág Estate.

Frank Gargiulo prepared the illustrations for *The Man Whose Trade Was Tricks*.

Marilee Heyer prepared the illustrations for *The Selkie Girl*.

Mary Jones prepared the illustrations for *The Monster Who Grew Small*.

Rosalind Kaye prepared the illustrations for *The Banza*.

Barry Moser's illustrations for *The Mushroom Man* are from the book of the same name by Ethel Pochocki. Copyright © 1993 by Barry Moser.

Jane Tattersfield prepared the illustrations for *The Princess and the Beggar*.

Cover art by Vivienne Flesher. Copyright © 2006 by Vivienne Flesher.

Text and cover design by William Seabright & Associates.

Interior design by Think Design Group.